Picture-Word Quizzes Assessment Sheets & Solutions

For The Children's Picture-Word & Simple Sentence Book

By

Dr. Harry R. Irving, Ed. D.

Cover Illustrations by Graphics Factory

Fully Reproducible

Primary Grades & ESOL Students

Order this book online at www.trafford.com
or email orders@trafford.com

Most Trafford titles are also available at major online book retailers.

Note for Librarians: A cataloguing record for this book is available from Library
and Archives Canada at www.collectionscanada.ca/amicus/index-e.html

Printed in Victoria, BC, Canada.

ISBN: 978-1-4269-0667-1 (Soft)
ISBN: 978-1-4269-0669-5 (e-book)

*Our mission is to efficiently provide the world's finest, most comprehensive
book publishing service, enabling every author to experience success.
To find out how to publish your book, your way, and have it available
worldwide, visit us online at www.trafford.com*

Trafford rev. 9/14/2009

 www.trafford.com

North America & international
toll-free: 1 888 232 4444 (USA & Canada)
phone: 250 383 6864 ♦ fax: 812 355 4082

Table of Contents

Picture-Word Quizzes (18)

Introduction

Purpose

The purpose of this book is threefold:

Primarily, this book is designed to assist parents and teachers in developing Children's Language Arts Skills, at home and at the school primary grade levels.

Secondarily, this assessment book, consisting of eighteen picture-word quizzes was developed by the author to accompany the author's " A Children's Picture-Word and Simple Sentence Book " and for the purpose of evaluating what the child has learned.

Thirdly, this book is designed for English for Speakers of Other Languages (ESOL) students.

Description

This assessment book consists of eighteen picture-word quizzes sheets, and solutions, ten questions per quiz, using the 180 pictures-words taken from the author's basic book, "A Children's Picture-Word and Simple Sentence Book".

Supplements

In addition to this assessment tool, the author has developed two additional assessment tools, (1) an eighteen word search and crossword puzzles assessment sheets book and (2) a 180 flip charts and name tags packet", also, for the purposes of measuring what the child has learned, and a children's picture coloring book", consisting of the 180 pictures of some animals and common things , that children will enjoy coloring, again, these supplements are designed to accompany the author's basic book, "A Children's Picture-Word and Simple Sentence Book".

Reproducible

The author grants teachers permission to photocopy the pages from this book for classroom use.

Finally, below is a list of the author's works that are a must and parents, teachers, and students are encouraged to purchase them. Each sold separately.

1) **"A Children's Picture-Word and Simple Sentence Book"**
2) **"Picture Coloring Book"**
3) **"Word Search and Crossword Puzzles Book"**
4) **"Picture-Word Quizzes Book"**
5) **"Flip Charts and Name Tags Packet"**

Name_____

Date_____

Quiz 1   ## Question 1 0f 10

Please darken in the bubble next to the correct answer.

Q.1) Find the word that matches this picture.

      O   A) car

      O   B) truck

      O   C) airplane

      O   D) bus

Name_____

Date_____

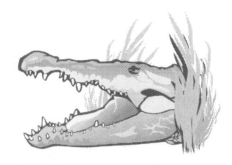

Please darken in the bubble next to the correct answer.

Q.2) Find the word that matches this picture.

        O A) dog

        O B) alligator

        O C) horse

        O D) cat

Name_____

Date_____

Please darken in the bubble next to the correct answer.

Q.3) Find the word that matches this picture.

○ A) ant

○ B) rat

○ C) snake

○ D) dog

Name_____

Date_____

Please darken in the bubble next to the correct answer.

Q.4) Find the word that matches this picture.

O A) cow

O B) dog

O C) bird

O D) ape

Name_____

Date_____

Please darken in the bubble next to the correct answer.

Q.5) Find the word that matches this picture.

O A) pear
O B) apple
O C) carrot
O D) orange

Name_____

Date_____

Please darken in the bubble next to the correct answer.

Q.6) Find the word that matches this picture.

○ A) balloon

○ B) ball

○ C) wagon

○ D) car

Name_____

Date_____

Please darken in the bubble next to the correct answer.

Q.7) Find the word that matches this picture.

        O A) balloons
        O B) kites
        O C) balls
        O D) airplanes

Name_____

Date_____

Please darken in the bubble next to the correct answer.

Q.8) Find the word that matches this picture.

    O A) oranges

    O B) apples

    O C) cherries

    O D) bananas

Name_____

Date_____

Please darken in the bubble next to the correct answer.

Q.9) Find the word that matches this picture.

        O A) bat

        O B) fly

        O C) butterfly

        O D) parrot

Name_____

Date_____

Please darken in the bubble next to the correct answer.

Q.10) Find the word that matches this picture.

        O A) cow

        O B) horse

        O C) bear

        O D) elephant

Name_____

Date_____

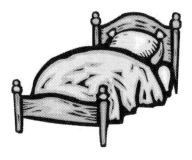

Quiz 2   **Question 1 0f 10**

Please darken in the bubble next to the correct answer.

Q.1) Find the word that matches this picture.

          O A) stove

          O B) bed

          O C) chair

          O D) table

Illustration by GraphicsFactory.com

Name_____

Date_____

Please darken in the bubble next to the correct answer.

Q.2) Find the word that matches this picture.

O A) car

O B) wagon

O C) boat

O D) bicycle

Name_____

Date_____

Please darken in the bubble next to the correct answer.

Q.3) Find the word that matches this picture.

        O A) bird

        O B) bat

        O C) parrot

        O D) cat

Name_____

Date_____

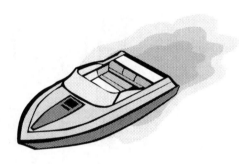

Please darken in the bubble next to the correct answer.

Q.4) Find the word that matches this picture.

       ◯ A) truck

       ◯ B) wagon

       ◯ C) boat

       ◯ D) car

Name_____

Date_____

Please darken in the bubble next to the correct answer.

Q.5) Find the word that matches this picture.

O A) book

O B) box

O C) door

O D) pencil

Name_____

Date_____

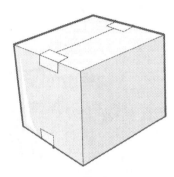

Please darken in the bubble next to the correct answer.

Q.6) Find the word that matches this picture.

O A) cake

O B) book

O C) box

O D) door

16

Name_____

Date_____

Please darken in the bubble next to the correct answer.

Q.7) Find the word that matches this picture.

O A) bowl

O B) fork

O C) glass

O D) pot

Name_____

Date_____

Please darken in the bubble next to the correct answer.

Q.8) Find the word that matches this picture.

        O A) boy

        O B) baby

        O C) butterfly

        O D) fox

Name_____

Date_____

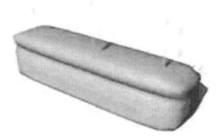

Please darken in the bubble next to the correct answer.

Q.9) Find the word that matches this picture.

O A) pie

O B) cake

O C) bread

O D) butter

Illustration by GraphicsFactory.com

Name_____

Date_____

Please darken in the bubble next to the correct answer.

Q.10) Find the word that matches this picture.

      O A) horse

      O B) buffalo

      O C) bear

      O D) sheep

Picture-Word Quiz

Name_____

Date_____

Quiz 3

Please darken in the bubble next to the correct answer.

Q.1) Find the word that matches this picture.

        ○ A) fly

        ○ B) snail

        ○ C) bug

        ○ D) butterfly

Name_____

Date_____

Please darken in the bubble next to the correct answer.

Q.2) Find the word that matches this picture.

       ○ A) train

       ○ B) car

       ○ C) truck

       ○ D) bus

Name_____

Date_____

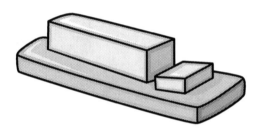

Please darken in the bubble next to the correct answer.

Q.3) Find the word that matches this picture.

      O A) butter

      O B) cheese

      O C) ice cream

      O D) cake

Illustration by GraphicsFactory.com

Name _____

Date _____

Please darken in the bubble next to the correct answer.

Q.4) Find the word that matches this picture.

O A) ant

O B) fly

O C) butterfly

O D) snail

Illustration by GraphicsFactory.com

Name_____

Date_____

Please darken in the bubble next to the correct answer.

Q.5) Find the word that matches this picture.

O A) bread

O B) cake

O C) pie

O D) hot dog

25

Name_____

Date_____

Please darken in the bubble next to the correct answer.

Q.6) Find the word that matches this picture.

        O A) elephant

        O B) kangaroo

        O C) cow

        O D) camel

Illustration by GraphicsFactory.com

Name_____

Date_____

Please darken in the bubble next to the correct answer.

Q.7) Find the word that matches this picture.

        O A) cup
        O B) cake
        O C) candle
        O D) glass

Illustration by GraphicsFactory.com

Name_____

Date_____

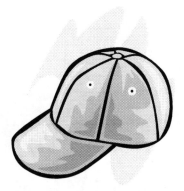

Please darken in the bubble next to the correct answer.

Q.8) Find the word that matches this picture.

      O A) jacket

      O B) cap

      O C) glove

      O D) shoe

Name_____

Date_____

Please darken in the bubble next to the correct answer.

Q.9) Find the word that matches this picture.

      O A) boat

      O B) truck

      O C) car

      O D) bus

Picture-Word Quiz

Name_____

Date_____

Please darken in the bubble next to the correct answer.

Q.10) Find the word that matches this picture.

　　　　　　　　O A) carrot

　　　　　　　　O B) apple

　　　　　　　　O C) pear

　　　　　　　　O D) peach

Name_____

Date_____

<u>Quiz 4</u>   **<u>Question 1 0f 10</u>**

Please darken in the bubble next to the correct answer.

Q.1) Find the word that matches this picture.

          ○ A) goat

          ○ B) cat

          ○ C) bat

          ○ D) cow

Illustration by GraphicsFactory.com

31

Name_____

Date_____

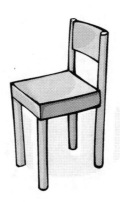

Please darken in the bubble next to the correct answer.

Q.2) Find the word that matches this picture.

       O A) table

       O B) couch

       O C) bed

       O D) chair

Name_____

Date_____

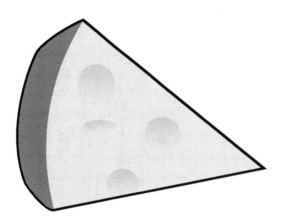

Please darken in the bubble next to the correct answer.

Q.3) Find the word that matches this picture.

        O A) hot dog

        O B) pie

        O C) cheese

        O D) cake

Illustration by GraphicsFactory.com

Name_____

Date_____

Please darken in the bubble next to the correct answer.

Q.4) Find the word that matches this picture.

        O A) carrot

        O B) hot dog

        O C) cake

        O D) cheeseburger

Name_____

Date_____

Please darken in the bubble next to the correct answer.

Q.5) Find the word that matches this picture.

O A) cherries

O B) oranges

O C) pears

O D) pineapples

Name_____

Date_____

Please darken in the bubble next to the correct answer.

Q.6) Find the word that matches this picture.

O A) bat

O B) rat

O C) chicken

O D) duck

Name_____

Date_____

Please darken in the bubble next to the correct answer.

Q.7) Find the word that matches this picture.

        ○ A) church

        ○ B) school

        ○ C) house

        ○ D) fence

Illustration by GraphicsFactory.com

Name_____

Date_____

Please darken in the bubble next to the correct answer.

Q.8) Find the word that matches this picture.

      O A) carrot

      O B) candle

      O C) cigarette

      O D) pencil

Name_____

Date_____

Please darken in the bubble next to the correct answer.

Q.9) Find the word that matches this picture.

       O A) telephone

       O B) clock

       O C) radio

       O D) television

Illustration by GraphicsFactory.com

Name_____

Date_____

Please darken in the bubble next to the correct answer.

Q.10) Find the word that matches this picture.

    O A) computer

    O B) wagon

    O C) book

    O D) chair

Illustration by GraphicsFactory.com

Name_____

Date_____

Quiz 5   **Question 1 0f 10**

Please darken in the bubble next to the correct answer.

Q.1) Find the word that matches this picture.

○ A) apples

○ B) bread

○ C) oranges

○ D) cookies

Illustration by GraphicsFactory.com

Name_____

Date_____

Please darken in the bubble next to the correct answer.

Q.2) Find the word that matches this picture.

        O   A)   table

        O   B)   bed

        O   C)   couch

        O   D)   chair

Name_____

Date_____

Please darken in the bubble next to the correct answer.

Q.3) Find the word that matches this picture.

     O A) cow

     O B) horse

     O C) goat

     O D) sheep

Illustration by GraphicsFactory.com

Name_____

Date_____

Please darken in the bubble next to the correct answer.

Q.4) Find the word that matches this picture.

◯ A) glass

◯ B) plate

◯ C) bowl

◯ D) cup

Name_____

Date_____

Please darken in the bubble next to the correct answer.

Q.5) Find the word that matches this picture.

      O A) elephant

      O B) giraffe

      O C) buffalo

      O D) deer

Name_____

Date_____

Please darken in the bubble next to the correct answer.

Q.6) Find the word that matches this picture.

      O A) dog

      O B) cat

      O C) tiger

      O D) rat

Name_____

Date_____

Please darken in the bubble next to the correct answer.

Q.7) Find the word that matches this picture.

O A) teddy-bear

O B) monkey

O C) doll

O D) puppy

Illustration by GraphicsFactory.com

Name_____

Date_____

Please darken in the bubble next to the correct answer.

Q.8) Find the word that matches this picture.

        O A) whale

        O B) dolphin

        O C) fish

        O D) jellyfish

Name_____

Date_____

Please darken in the bubble next to the correct answer.

Q.9) Find the word that matches this picture.

O   A)   house

O   B)   fence

O   C)   door

O   D)   window

Illustration by GraphicsFactory.com

Name_____

Date_____

Please darken in the bubble next to the correct answer.

Q.10) Find the word that matches this picture.

O A) jacket

O B) dress

O C) hat

O D) cap

Name_____

Date_____

Quiz 6   **Question 1 0f 10**

Please darken in the bubble next to the correct answer.

Q.1) Find the word that matches this picture.

           O A) car

           O B) drums

           O C) tree

           O D) ape

Name_____

Date_____

Please darken in the bubble next to the correct answer.

Q.2) Find the word that matches this picture.

       O A) goat

       O B) cow

       O C) rabbit

       O D) duck

Name_____

Date_____

Please darken in the bubble next to the correct answer.

Q.3) Find the word that matches this picture.

　　　　　　　　　　　○　A)　eagle

　　　　　　　　　　　○　B)　snail

　　　　　　　　　　　○　C)　zebra

　　　　　　　　　　　○　D)　parrot

Name_____

Date_____

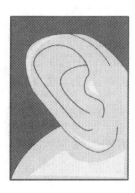

Please darken in the bubble next to the correct answer.

Q.4) Find the word that matches this picture.

○ A) finger

○ B) leg

○ C) ear

○ D) eye

54

Name_____

Date_____

Please darken in the bubble next to the correct answer.

Q.5) Find the word that matches this picture.

        O A) eggs

        O B) milk

        O C) bread

        O D) cheese

Name_____

Date_____

Please darken in the bubble next to the correct answer.

Q.6) Find the word that matches this picture.

     ○ A) one
     ○ B) five
     ○ C) six
     ○ D) eight

Name_____

Date_____

Please darken in the bubble next to the correct answer.

Q.7) Find the word that matches this picture.

      O A) bear

      O B) elephant

      O C) horse

      O D) lion

Illustration by GraphicsFactory.com

Name_____

Date_____

Please darken in the bubble next to the correct answer.

Q.8) Find the word that matches this picture.

    O A) nose

    O B) ear

    O C) eye

    O D) lip

Illustration by GraphicsFactory.com

Name_____

Date_____

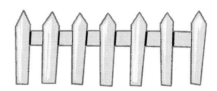

Please darken in the bubble next to the correct answer.

Q.9) Find the word that matches this picture.

O A) fence
O B) house
O C) door
O D) water

Name_____

Date_____

Please darken in the bubble next to the correct answer.

Q.10) Find the word that matches this picture.

        O A) sky

        O B) fire

        O C) bug

        O D) star

Name_____

Date_____

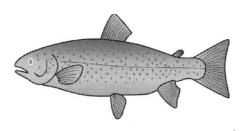

Quiz 7   **Question 1 0f 10**

Please darken in the bubble next to the correct answer.

Q.1) Find the word that matches this picture.

O   A)   snail
O   B)   shrimp
O   C)   frog
O   D)   fish

Name_____

Date_____

Please darken in the bubble next to the correct answer.

Q.2) Find the word that matches this picture.

        O A)   two

        O B)   five

        O C)   four

        O D)   three

Name_____

Date_____

Please darken in the bubble next to the correct answer.

Q.3) Find the word that matches this picture.

O A) flag
O B) kite
O C) money
O D) book

Name_____

Date_____

Please darken in the bubble next to the correct answer.

Q.4) Find the word that matches this picture.

        O A) flower

        O B) potato

        O C) tomato

        O D) tree

Name_____

Date_____

Please darken in the bubble next to the correct answer.

Q.5) Find the word that matches this picture.

O A) butterfly

O B) ant

O C) flag

O D) fly

Name_____

Date _____

Please darken in the bubble next to the correct answer.

Q.6) Find the word that matches this picture.

    O A) spoon

    O B) fork

    O C) knife

    O D) cup

Illustration by GraphicsFactory.com

Name_____

Date_____

Please darken in the bubble next to the correct answer.

Q.7) Find the word that matches this picture.

        O A) two

        O B) four

        O C) six

        O D) eight

Illustration by GraphicsFactory.com

Name_____

Date_____

Please darken in the bubble next to the correct answer.

Q.8) Find the word that matches this picture.

      O A) cat

      O B) lion

      O C) leopard

      O D) fox

Name_____

Date_____

Please darken in the bubble next to the correct answer.

Q.9) Find the word that matches this picture.

O A) cookies

O B) French fries

O C) hamburger

O D) soda

Name_____

Date_____

Please darken in the bubble next to the correct answer.

Q.10) Find the word that matches this picture.

    O A) rat

    O B) dog

    O C) frog

    O D) lizard

Illustration by GraphicsFactory.com

Picture-Word Quiz

Name_____

Date_____

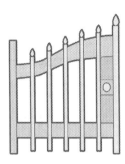

Quiz 8   **Question 1 0f 10**

Please darken in the bubble next to the correct answer.

Q.1) Find the word that matches this picture.

            O   A)   gate
            O   B)   door
            O   C)   fence
            O   D)   window

Name_____

Date_____

Please darken in the bubble next to the correct answer.

Q.2) Find the word that matches this picture.

        O A) buffalo

        O B) elephant

        O C) tiger

        O D) giraffe

Illustration by GraphicsFactory.com

Name_____

Date_____

Please darken in the bubble next to the correct answer.

Q.3) Find the word that matches this picture.

      O A) girl

      O B) rabbit

      O C) kitten

      O D) duck

Illustration by GraphicsFactory.com

Name_____

Date_____

Please darken in the bubble next to the correct answer.

Q.4) Find the word that matches this picture.

    O A) glass

    O B) plate

    O C) bowl

    O D) cup

Illustration by GraphicsFactory.com

Name_____

Date_____

Please darken in the bubble next to the correct answer.

Q.5) Find the word that matches this picture.

      O A) hat

      O B) shoes

      O C) gloves

      O D) cap

Name_____

Date_____

Please darken in the bubble next to the correct answer.

Q.6) Find the word that matches this picture.

O A) sheep

O B) goat

O C) pig

O D) bear

Name_____

Date_____

Please darken in the bubble next to the correct answer.

Q.7) Find the word that matches this picture.

       O A) oranges

       O B) pears

       O C) apples

       O D) grapes

Illustration by GraphicsFactory.com

Name_____

Date_____

Please darken in the bubble next to the correct answer.

Q.8) Find the word that matches this picture.

      O A) wagon

      O B) gun

      O C) car

      O D) train

Illustration by GraphicsFactory.com

Name_____

Date_____

Please darken in the bubble next to the correct answer.

Q.9) Find the word that matches this picture.

      O A) popcorn

      O B) hot dog

      O C) hamburger

      O D) chicken

Illustration by GraphicsFactory.com

Name_____

Date_____

Please darken in the bubble next to the correct answer.

Q.10) Find the word that matches this picture.

O A) dress

O B) shirt

O C) socks

O D) hat

Name_____

Date_____

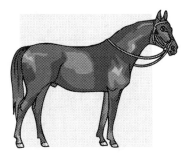

Quiz 9   **Question 1 0f 10**

Please darken in the bubble next to the correct answer.

Q.1) Find the word that matches this picture.

⭕ A) horse
⭕ B) giraffe
⭕ C) cow
⭕ D) buffalo

Illustration by GraphicsFactory.com

Name_____

Date_____

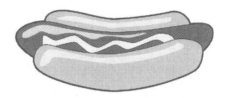

Please darken in the bubble next to the correct answer.

Q.2) Find the word that matches this picture.

       O A) cheeseburger

       O B) pizza

       O C) hot dog

       O D) carrot

Name_____

Date_____

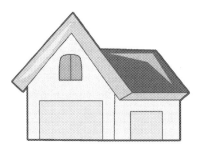

Please darken in the bubble next to the correct answer.

Q.3) Find the word that matches this picture.

       O A) car

       O B) house

       O C) truck

       O D) turkey

Illustration by GraphicsFactory.com

Name_____

Date_____

Please darken in the bubble next to the correct answer.

Q.4) Find the word that matches this picture.

      O A) ice cream

      O B) jell-O

      O C) cake

      O D) pudding

Name_____

Date_____

Please darken in the bubble next to the correct answer.

Q.5) Find the word that matches this picture.

       O A) cap

       O B) gloves

       O C) jacket

       O D) dress

Illustration by GraphicsFactory.com

Name_____

Date_____

Please darken in the bubble next to the correct answer.

Q.6) Find the word that matches this picture.

O A) snake

O B) snail

O C) whale

O D) jellyfish

Name_____

Date_____

Please darken in the bubble next to the correct answer.

Q.7) Find the word that matches this picture.

O A) water

O B) juice

O C) milk

O D) tea

Name_____

Date_____

Please darken in the bubble next to the correct answer.

Q.8) Find the word that matches this picture.

- ○ A) kangaroo
- ○ B) giraffe
- ○ C) monkey
- ○ D) horse

Name_____

Date_____

Please darken in the bubble next to the correct answer.

Q.9) Find the word that matches this picture.

○ A) kite

○ B) key

○ C) knife

○ D) fork

Name_____

Date_____

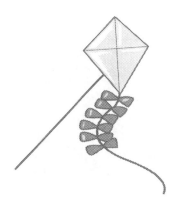

Please darken in the bubble next to the correct answer.

Q.10) Find the word that matches this picture.

        O A) airplane

        O B) bird

        O C) jacket

        O D) kite

Picture-Word Quiz

Name_____

Date_____

Quiz 10

Please darken in the bubble next to the correct answer.

Q.1) Find the word that matches this picture.

O A) kitten

O B) puppy

O C) dog

O D) duck

Illustration by GraphicsFactory.com

Name_____

Date_____

Please darken in the bubble next to the correct answer.

Q.2) Find the word that matches this picture.

○ A) spoon

○ B) fork

○ C) knife

○ D) key

Name_____

Date_____

Please darken in the bubble next to the correct answer.

Q.3) Find the word that matches this picture.

        ○ A) ladder

        ○ B) lamp

        ○ C) table

        ○ D) chair

Illustration by GraphicsFactory.com

Name_____

Date_____

Please darken in the bubble next to the correct answer.

Q.4) Find the word that matches this picture.

       O A) clock

       O B) radio

       O C) telephone

       O D) lamp

Name_____

Date_____

Please darken in the bubble next to the correct answer.

Q.5) Find the word that matches this picture.

       O A) lemon

       O B) orange

       O C) apple

       O D) pear

Illustration by GraphicsFactory.com

Name_____

Date_____

Please darken in the bubble next to the correct answer.

Q.6) Find the word that matches this picture.

O A) lion

O B) bear

O C) horse

O D) leopard

Name_____

Date_____

Please darken in the bubble next to the correct answer.

Q.7) Find the word that matches this picture.

        O A) tomato

        O B) lettuce

        O C) carrot

        O D) potato

Illustration by GraphicsFactory.com

Name_____

Date_____

Please darken in the bubble next to the correct answer.

Q.8) Find the word that matches this picture.

      ○ A) lion
      ○ B) tiger
      ○ C) buffalo
      ○ D) elephant

Illustration by GraphicsFactory.com

Name_____

Date_____

Please darken in the bubble next to the correct answer.

Q.9) Find the word that matches this picture.

       O A) snake

       O B) turtle

       O C) frog

       O D) lizard

Name_____

Date_____

Please darken in the bubble next to the correct answer.

Q.10) Find the word that matches this picture.

       O A) man

       O B) apple

       O C) kitten

       O D) cherry

Illustration by GraphicsFactory.com

Name_____

Date_____

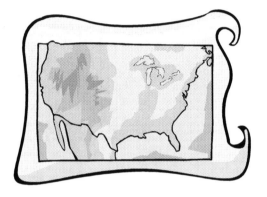

Quiz 11   **Question 1 0f 10**

Please darken in the bubble next to the correct answer.

Q.1) Find the word that matches this picture.

    O A) book

    O B) flower

    O C) map

    O D) clock

Illustration by GraphicsFactory.com

Name_____

Date_____

Please darken in the bubble next to the correct answer.

Q.2) Find the word that matches this picture.

        O A) coffee

        O B) milk

        O C) juice

        O D) soda

Illustration by GraphicsFactory.com

Name_____

Date_____

Please darken in the bubble next to the correct answer.

Q.3) Find the word that matches this picture.

      O A) money

      O B) lettuce

      O C) bread

      O D) book

Name_____

Date_____

Please darken in the bubble next to the correct answer.

Q.4) Find the word that matches this picture.

      O   A)   zebra

      O   B)   raccoon

      O   C)   dog

      O   D)   monkey

Illustration by GraphicsFactory.com

Name_____

Date_____

Please darken in the bubble next to the correct answer.

Q.5) Find the word that matches this picture.

       O A) buffalo

       O B) elephant

       O C) moose

       O D) horse

Illustration by GraphicsFactory.com

Name_____

Date_____

Please darken in the bubble next to the correct answer.

Q.6) Find the word that matches this picture.

        O A) motorcycle

        O B) car

        O C) bus

        O D) wagon

Illustration by GraphicsFactory.com

Name_____

Date_____

Please darken in the bubble next to the correct answer.

Q.7) Find the word that matches this picture.

      ○ A) puppy

      ○ B) squirrel

      ○ C) duck

      ○ D) mouse

Illustration by GraphicsFactory.com

Name_____

Date_____

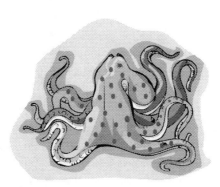

Please darken in the bubble next to the correct answer.

Q.8) Find the word that matches this picture.

O A) octopus

O B) jellyfish

O C) whale

O D) tiger

Illustration by GraphicsFactory.com

Name_____

Date_____

Please darken in the bubble next to the correct answer.

Q.9) Find the word that matches this picture.

    O A) ten

    O B) 0ne

    O C) eleven

    O D) four

Illustration by GraphicsFactory.com

Name_____

Date_____

Please darken in the bubble next to the correct answer.

Q.10) Find the word that matches this picture.

○ A) apple

○ B) peach

○ C) orange

○ D) pear

Name_____

Date_____

Quiz 12   **Question 1 0f 10**

Please darken in the bubble next to the correct answer.

Q.1) Find the word that matches this picture.

        O A) owl

        O B) parrot

        O C) bat

        O D) duck

Name_____

Date_____

Please darken in the bubble next to the correct answer.

Q.2) Find the word that matches this picture.

       O A) pot

       O B) pan

       O C) plate

       O D) pencil

Name_____

Date_____

Please darken in the bubble next to the correct answer.

Q.3) Find the word that matches this picture.

O A) shirts

O B) skirts

O C) pants

O D) socks

Illustration by GraphicsFactory.com

Name_____

Date_____

Please darken in the bubble next to the correct answer.

Q.4) Find the word that matches this picture.

      ○ A) parrot

      ○ B) chicken

      ○ C) owl

      ○ D) monkey

Name_____

Date_____

Please darken in the bubble next to the correct answer.

Q.5) Find the word that matches this picture.

      O A) apple

      O B) peach

      O C) cherry

      O D) pear

Illustration by GraphicsFactory.com

Name_____

Date_____

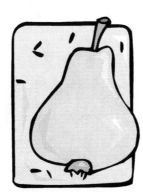

Please darken in the bubble next to the correct answer.

Q.6) Find the word that matches this picture.

O A) pear
O B) apple
O C) peach
O D) orange

Name_____

Date_____

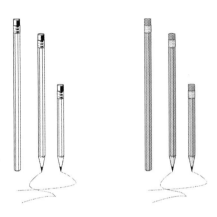

Please darken in the bubble next to the correct answer.

Q.7) Find the word that matches this picture.

      ○ A) pants

      ○ B) plates

      ○ C) pans

      ○ D) pencils

Name_____

Date_____

Please darken in the bubble next to the correct answer.

Q.8) Find the word that matches this picture.

　　　　　　　　O A) piano
　　　　　　　　O B) table
　　　　　　　　O C) chair
　　　　　　　　O D) couch

Illustration by GraphicsFactory.com

Name_____

Date_____

Please darken in the bubble next to the correct answer.

Q.9) Find the word that matches this picture.

O A) cake

O B) pie

O C) pizza

O D) bread

Name_____

Date_____

Please darken in the bubble next to the correct answer.

Q.10) Find the word that matches this picture.

       O A) sheep

       O B) goat

       O C) pig

       O D) cat

Illustration by GraphicsFactory.com

Name_____

Date_____

Quiz 13   **Question 1 0f 10**

Please darken in the bubble next to the correct answer.

Q.1) Find the word that matches this picture.

        O A) pineapple

        O B) banana

        O C) potato

        O D) apple

Illustration by GraphicsFactory.com

Name_____

Date_____

Please darken in the bubble next to the correct answer.

Q.2) Find the word that matches this picture.

        O A) bread

        O B) cake

        O C) pizza

        O D) hot dog

Illustration by GraphicsFactory.com

Name_____

Date_____

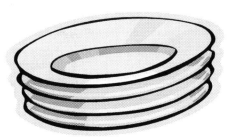

Please darken in the bubble next to the correct answer.

Q.3) Find the word that matches this picture.

        ○ A) cups

        ○ B) glasses

        ○ C) pans

        ○ D) plates

Illustration by GraphicsFactory.com

Name_____

Date_____

Please darken in the bubble next to the correct answer.

Q.4) Find the word that matches this picture.

        O A) pool table

        O B) couch

        O C) chair

        O D) door

Name_____

Date_____

Please darken in the bubble next to the correct answer.

Q.5) Find the word that matches this picture.

O A) plate

O B) pot

O C) pan

O D) table

Name_____

Date_____

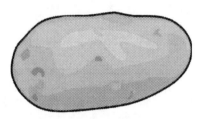

Please darken in the bubble next to the correct answer.

Q.6) Find the word that matches this picture.

       O A) potato

       O B) tomato

       O C) orange

       O D) cookie

Name_____

Date_____

Please darken in the bubble next to the correct answer.

Q.7) Find the word that matches this picture.

O A) pineapple

O B) pumpkin

O C) flower

O D) potato

Name_____

Date_____

Please darken in the bubble next to the correct answer.

Q.8) Find the word that matches this picture.

      O A) rabbit

      O B) duck

      O C) puppy

      O D) kitten

Name_____

Date_____

Please darken in the bubble next to the correct answer.

Q.9) Find the word that matches this picture.

        O A) bear

        O B) rabbit

        O C) mouse

        O D) duck

Name_____

Date_____

Please darken in the bubble next to the correct answer.

Q.10) Find the word that matches this picture.

      O A) raccoon

      O B) fox

      O C) deer

      O D) sheep

Name_____

Date_____

Quiz 14   **Question 1 0f 10**

Please darken in the bubble next to the correct answer.

Q.1) Find the word that matches this picture.

           O   A)   telephone

           O   B)   television

           O   C)   radio

           O   D)   computer

Name_____

Date_____

Please darken in the bubble next to the correct answer.

Q.2) Find the word that matches this picture.

      O A) rat

      O B) squirrel

      O C) cat

      O D) dog

Name_____

Date_____

Please darken in the bubble next to the correct answer.

Q.3) Find the word that matches this picture.

O A) cup

O B) pan

O C) car

O D) ring

Name_____

Date_____

Please darken in the bubble next to the correct answer.

Q.4) Find the word that matches this picture.

       ○ A) school

       ○ B) box

       ○ C) bus

       ○ D) train

Name_____

Date_____

Please darken in the bubble next to the correct answer.

Q.5) Find the word that matches this picture.

        O A) lion

        O B) snail

        O C) seal

        O D) tiger

Name_____

Date_____

Please darken in the bubble next to the correct answer.

Q.6) Find the word that matches this picture.

○ A) four

○ B) five

○ C) six

○ D) seven

Illustration by GraphicsFactory.com

Name_____

Date_____

Please darken in the bubble next to the correct answer.

Q.7) Find the word that matches this picture.

○ A) shark

○ B) dolphin

○ C) boat

○ D) jellyfish

Name_____

Date_____

Please darken in the bubble next to the correct answer.

Q.8) Find the word that matches this picture.

       O A) tiger

       O B) bear

       O C) sheep

       O D) raccoon

Name_____

Date_____

Please darken in the bubble next to the correct answer.

Q.9) Find the word that matches this picture.

O A) ship
O B) bus
O C) train
O D) truck

Name_____

Date_____

Please darken in the bubble next to the correct answer.

Q.10) Find the word that matches this picture.

      O A) dress

      O B) shirt

      O C) jacket

      O D) skirt

Picture-Word Quiz

Name_____

Date_____

Quiz 15

Please darken in the bubble next to the correct answer.

Q.1) Find the word that matches this picture.

        O   A)   shoes

        O   B)   socks

        O   C)   pants

        O   D)   shirts

Illustration by GraphicsFactory.com

Name_____

Date_____

Please darken in the bubble next to the correct answer.

Q.2) Find the word that matches this picture.

       O A) three

       O B) four

       O C) five

       O D) six

Name_____

Date_____

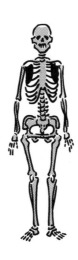

Please darken in the bubble next to the correct answer.

Q.3) Find the word that matches this picture.

　　　　　　　　○ A) tree
　　　　　　　　○ B) ape
　　　　　　　　○ C) skeleton
　　　　　　　　○ D) monkey

Name_____

Date_____

Please darken in the bubble next to the correct answer.

Q.4) Find the word that matches this picture.

O A) skirt

O B) shirt

O C) jacket

O D) dress

Name_____

Date_____

Please darken in the bubble next to the correct answer.

Q.5) Find the word that matches this picture.

       ○ A) rat

       ○ B) skunk

       ○ C) rabbit

       ○ D) deer

Name_____

Date_____

Please darken in the bubble next to the correct answer.

Q.6) Find the word that matches this picture.

O A) sun

O B) stars

O C) book

O D) pie

Name_____

Date_____

Please darken in the bubble next to the correct answer.

Q.7) Find the word that matches this picture.

O   A)   snail

O   B)   turtle

O   C)   fly

O   D)   rat

Name_____

Date_____

Please darken in the bubble next to the correct answer.

Q.8) Find the word that matches this picture.

      O A) mouse

      O B) squirrel

      O C) snake

      O D) bird

Name_____

Date_____

Please darken in the bubble next to the correct answer.

Q.9) Find the word that matches this picture.

         O A) shoes

         O B) socks

         O C) pants

         O D) shirts

Name_____

Date_____

Please darken in the bubble next to the correct answer.

Q.1o) Find the word that matches this picture.

○ A) spoon

○ B) knife

○ C) fork

○ D) pencil

Picture-Word Quiz

Name_____

Date_____

Quiz 16   **Question 1 0f 10**

Please darken in the bubble next to the correct answer.

Q.1) Find the word that matches this picture.

        O A) rat

        O B) squirrel

        O C) rabbit

        O D) cat

Name_____

Date_____

Please darken in the bubble next to the correct answer.

Q.2) Find the word that matches this picture.

        O A) computer

        O B) table

        O C) radio

        O D) stove

Illustration by GraphicsFactory.com

Name_____

Date_____

Please darken in the bubble next to the correct answer.

Q.3) Find the word that matches this picture.

     O A) sun

     O B) moon

     O C) orange

     O D) doll

Illustration by GraphicsFactory.com

Name_____

Date_____

Please darken in the bubble next to the correct answer.

Q.4) Find the word that matches this picture.

      O A) pan

      O B) plate

      O C) sunglasses

      O D) eye

Name_____

Date_____

Please darken in the bubble next to the correct answer.

Q.5) Find the word that matches this picture.

O A) swimming pool

O B) gate

O C) fence

O D) school

Name _____

Date _____

Please darken in the bubble next to the correct answer.

Q.6) Find the word that matches this picture.

○ A) chair

○ B) table

○ C) couch

○ D) bed

Name_____

Date_____

Please darken in the bubble next to the correct answer.

Q.7) Find the word that matches this picture.

O A) teddy-bear

O B) monkey

O C) ape

O D) cat

Name_____

Date_____

Please darken in the bubble next to the correct answer.

Q.8) Find the word that matches this picture.

      O A) radio

      O B) telephone

      O C) computer

      O D) television

Name_____

Date_____

Please darken in the bubble next to the correct answer.

Q.9) Find the word that matches this picture.

○ A) telephone

○ B) radio

○ C) stove

○ D) television

Name_____

Date_____

Please darken in the bubble next to the correct answer.

Q.10) Find the word that matches this picture.

O A) seven

O B) eight

O C) nine

O D) ten

Illustration by GraphicsFactory.com

Picture-Word Quiz

Name_____

Date_____

Quiz 17

Please darken in the bubble next to the correct answer.

Q.1) Find the word that matches this picture.

       O A) one
       O B) two
       O C) three
       O D) four

Illustration by GraphicsFactory.com

Name_____

Date_____

Please darken in the bubble next to the correct answer.

Q.2) Find the word that matches this picture.

      O A) lion

      O B) tiger

      O C) leopard

      O D) deer

Illustration by GraphicsFactory.com

Name_____

Date_____

Please darken in the bubble next to the correct answer.

Q.3) Find the word that matches this picture.

O A) tomato

O B) potato

O C) apple

O D) orange

Name_____

Date_____

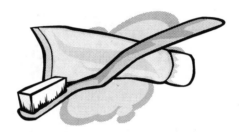

Please darken in the bubble next to the correct answer.

Q.4) Find the word that matches this picture.

O A) pencil

O B) toothbrush

O C) spoon

O D) knife

Name_____

Date_____

Please darken in the bubble next to the correct answer.

Q.5) Find the word that matches this picture.

O A) bus
O B) train
O C) car
O D) wagon

Name_____

Date_____

Please darken in the bubble next to the correct answer.

Q.6) Find the word that matches this picture.

O   A) tree
O   B) three
O   C) flower
O   D) pencil

Name_____

Date_____

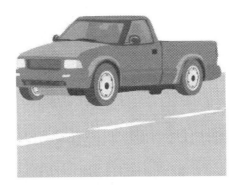

Please darken in the bubble next to the correct answer.

Q.7) Find the word that matches this picture.

O A) car

O B) bus

O C) truck

O D) motorcycle

Name_____

Date_____

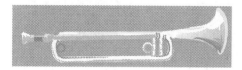

Please darken in the bubble next to the correct answer.

Q.8) Find the word that matches this picture.

O A) trumpet

O B) piano

O C) drums

O D) telephone

Name_____

Date_____

Please darken in the bubble next to the correct answer.

Q.9) Find the word that matches this picture.

O   A) turtle

O   B) turkey

O   C) chicken

O   D) rabbit

Name_____

Date_____

Please darken in the bubble next to the correct answer.

Q.10) Find the word that matches this picture.

O A) snail

O B) raccoon

O C) turtle

O D) lizard

Name_____

Date_____

<u>Quiz 18</u>   **<u>Question 1 0f 10</u>**

Please darken in the bubble next to the correct answer.

Q.1) Find the word that matches this picture.

         O A) one
         O B) two
         O C) three
         O D) four

Name_____

Date_____

Please darken in the bubble next to the correct answer.

Q.2) Find the word that matches this picture.

      O A) umbrella

      O B) book

      O C) chair

      O D) dress

Name_____

Date_____

Please darken in the bubble next to the correct answer.

Q.3) Find the word that matches this picture.

       O A) vase

       O B) flower

       O C) chair

       O D) table

Name_____

Date_____

Please darken in the bubble next to the correct answer.

Q.4) Find the word that matches this picture.

      O A) pot

      O B) pineapple

      O C) volcano

      O D) map

Illustration by GraphicsFactory.com

Name_____

Date_____

Please darken in the bubble next to the correct answer.

Q.5) Find the word that matches this picture.

        O A) boat

        O B) car

        O C) truck

        O D) wagon

Name_____

Date_____

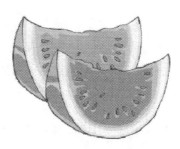

Please darken in the bubble next to the correct answer.

Q.6) Find the word that matches this picture.

      O A) watermelon

      O B) orange

      O C) pizza

      O D) bread

Name_____

Date_____

Please darken in the bubble next to the correct answer.

Q.7) Find the word that matches this picture.

       O A) sheep

       O B) whale

       O C) tiger

       O D) cow

Name_____

Date_____

Please darken in the bubble next to the correct answer.

Q.8) Find the word that matches this picture.

     O A) door

     O B) window

     O C) gate

     O D) fence

Name_____

Date_____

Please darken in the bubble next to the correct answer.

Q.9) Find the word that matches this picture.

O A) woman & baby

O B) cat & dog

O C) apple & orange

O D) flower & pot

Name_____

Date_____

Please darken in the bubble next to the correct answer.

Q.10) Find the word that matches this picture.

○ A) horse

○ B) cow

○ C) dog

○ D) zebra

Picture-Word Quiz

Name_____

Date_____

Solutions

Quiz 1	**Quiz 2**	**Quiz 3**	**Quiz 4**
1C	1B	1C	1B
2B	2D	2D	2D
3A	3A	3A	3C
4D	4C	4C	4D
5B	5A	5B	5A
6B	6C	6D	6C
7A	7A	7C	7A
8D	8A	8B	8C
9A	9C	9C	9B
10C	10B	10A	10A

Quiz 5	**Quiz 6**	**Quiz 7**	**Quiz 8**
1D	1B	1 D	1A
2C	2D	2 B	2D
3A	3A	3 A	3A
4D	4C	4 A	4A
5D	5A	5 D	5C
6A	6D	6 B	6B
7C	7B	7 B	7D
8B	8C	8 D	8B
9C	9A	9 B	9C
10B	10B	10 C	10D

Name_____

Date_____

Solutions

Quiz 9	Quiz 10	Quiz 11	Quiz 12
1A	1A	1C	1A
2C	2C	2B	2B
3B	3A	3A	3C
4A	4D	4D	4A
5C	5A	5C	5B
6D	6D	6A	6C
7B	7B	7D	7D
8A	8A	8A	8A
9B	9D	9B	9B
10D	10A	10C	10C

Quiz 13	Quiz 14	Quiz 15	Quiz 16
1A	1C	1A	1B
2C	2A	2D	2D
3D	3D	3C	3A
4A	4A	4A	4C
5B	5C	5B	5A
6A	6D	6B	6B
7B	7A	7A	7A
8C	8C	8C	8B
9B	9A	9B	9D
10A	10B	10A	10D

Name_____

Date_____

Solutions

Quiz 17	**Quiz 18**
1C	1B
2B	2A
3A	3A
4B	4C
5B	5D
6A	6A
7C	7B
8A	8B
9A	9A
10C	10D